Introduction

This book is aimed at young people in year nine who are going to have to make decisions and choices about their future.

Thank you for choosing this book. Congratulations too as you have now acknowledged that your desire is to get the best from your life by deciding what you would like in your future. This book will help you to identify the journey for the future whatever route you choose to take. I hope you enjoy working through this book it has been designed to help you to get started on your future career whatever route you choose. It will take you through some practical exercises which will help you to explore what you want and where you would like to be in the future.

Are you worried about your future?

Are you concerned you are not going to get a job?

Does your mind go blank when people ask you what you want to do?

You are not alone. I had similar experiences when I was at school and both my children had quite different experiences. So read on and enjoy the journey of making decisions and choices that are right for you.

What prompted me to write this book?

By coaching unemployed people back into work and the work I have undertaken in schools with young people I recognised that young people like you would benefit from coaching to help you make decisions about your life. Once you move on to secondary school you realise that you now have to start to make decisions about your future. I have recognised that the transition for some of you is moving from school into the big wide world can be quite daunting and you just don't know where to start. The school environment has become to some within your comfort zone and this will soon come to an end. The comfort zone is a place where you feel safe, comfortable and everything you do is second nature. Being in your comfort zone enables you to be confident but to help you to grow as an individual sometimes you need to push those boundaries to try new and exciting experiences. Within school you will have learned to have recognised which subjects you are really good at and which ones you are not so good at. Whatever you choose to do now may have some impact on your confidence as you are about to learn about a new environment and develop even more knowledge and skills which will take you out of your comfort zone. This can create some element of fear. Exploring yourself by working through this book may also take you out of your comfort zone.

What we as adults expect you to know is what you want to do when you leave school. Some of you may be very clear on where your future career direction is going and for others the question is still unanswered. When I think back to when I was sixteen I was not aware of all the different career paths that were there in the big wide world. Yet when we choose our subjects for our final years at school we may not really know what it is we want to do. My career has evolved over many years and moved on with the opportunities that have presented themselves to me.

As a Youth Worker and a mother to two children, who are now grown up. I have gained an understanding of the difficulties that young people are faced with when making choices about their future. How you deal with making decisions can depend on the support that you have available to you and whether you are in touch with people that are also motivated and positive.

I want to use my experience of personal development and share this with all you young people out there. I want you to get the best out of your life and have a clear focus to enable you to develop a plan. My daughter had a very clear career direction of going into nursing. She did extremely well at school was very focused and motivated. She achieved what she wanted.

For my son it was a different story. He had no clear focus on his future career and did well in his achievements but he had no passion there in what he was doing. After receiving career advice at school he went to university to study to be a solicitor. When he told me what he had chosen to do I knew it was not for him as he wasn't keen on studying and his passion was science. I had to allow him to find out for himself. He lasted three weeks at university and dropped out when he eventually realised it wasn't for him. He already had a part-time job in a large supermarket so decided to work full-time and undertake training to develop his career. Now in his late 20's he has recognised this is not the career for him and is currently pursuing other options.

Advice and support plays an important factor in the choices and decisions that you make. You need to find someone you trust, someone that will listen to you and also understand where your passion lies.

I would like all you young people to self-coach yourself using this book to enable you to identify the passion of what you are interested in and have the motivation and drive to succeed. It will help you to explore your career path, believe in yourself and maintain a positive mind set to get whatever you desire in your life.

When I was a teenager my thoughts on a career were influenced by my parents. My initial thoughts were about going into the Armed Forces as my father thought this was a good career. I also had a thought about being a teacher. By the time I left school I wanted to go to college to be a Nursery Nurse but as my mother worked in an office I was encouraged to take this route. As soon as I left school I was employed in a well paid job in an office but this never made me feel fulfilled. I found it boring as it wasn't enough of a challenge for me. Once I left to have my children at quite a young age felt this was my time for deciding the potential opportunities that I could pursue. Sometimes we need to take time to re-assess where we want to be and what we want to do.

As we spend a lot of our life working I think it is particularly important that we get the start of the journey right. That doesn't mean you can't just take any job. What it does mean is that you view what you do as part of the journey to getting one step nearer to where you want to be.

Throughout your life you will constantly be learning through the experiences that you have. Events happen in our lives which sometimes make us re-focus where we are and where we want to be.

When I was at school I worked on a Saturday in clothes shop which I enjoyed. I left school and worked as a Clerical Assistant until I had my children. I then needed a part time job and re-trained to be a Youth Worker I found this to be a fulfilling job. I wasn't aware until I was in this job that you could work full-time as a Youth & Community Worker. By going to university to study I achieved this. This opened my eyes to a whole host of organisations that supported people to overcome problems and issues in their lives. I have always been interested in helping others. I started to develop more of an interest in community development work. Whilst working in this field yet again I found other areas of interest. Throughout all of this I was increasing my knowledge and skills.

It wasn't until 2006 when I was made redundant that I realised that I had the skills and experience to be able to set up my own business. After applying for forty jobs using the knowledge I had gained through recruitment and selection training I was extremely successful in being invited for interviews. I did get back into employment but realised this was a means to an end as it was a short term contract. Whilst working full time I identified that I wanted to be a life coach to help others and re-trained to gain my Diploma in Personal Development Coaching and also a Diploma in Corporate and Executive Coaching.

I did something I had never done before and that was to stay in a job that I knew was coming to an end and was made redundant for a second time. I knew at this moment in time being self-employed is what I wanted to do. This was a big risk for me to take but I knew in my heart this is what I wanted.

As you can see from a brief description about my career path it can evolve over a period of time to enable you to identify where you want to be.

So don't worry if you are not sure what you want to do or where you want to be in the future. What is important is that you enjoy the journey along the way whilst you find what you are passionate about.

What you need to do is to have the confidence and self-belief along with the drive and the passion to get you to succeed in what you are happy with in your life both now and in the future.

This book will help you to get a good start by providing you with the tools and techniques to enable you to explore what opportunities are open to you.

How to read this book

This book has been written in a particular order and is best to be read in the sequence it is laid out in. To get the best from the book you need to undertake the exercises in each chapter. The exercises have been designed to challenge you to think and get to know yourself. The questions will help you to tap into your own intuition so allow the questions to bring out the truths you need to get what you want in your life.

Throughout the book there may be some repetition. This is intended and is part of the process. The repetition will help to remind you to continue with what you have learned in previous chapters.

Congratulations again for purchasing this book as it is the first step in your taking responsibility for you getting the best from your life and achieving what you want to achieve.

So, let's get started on this exciting exploration of what you want and how you can get it in your life.

Chapter 1

Knowing what you want to do

Are people constantly asking you, 'what do you want to do when you leave school?'

Is your response 'I don't know'?

Does leaving school make you feel anxious or quite excited?

So what are your potential options?

- Go to college to learn a skill for your future career.

- Apprenticeships

- Go to university study a subject related to your chosen career

- Set up a business

- Get a job – any job

Whatever your thoughts are you need to ensure you make the right decision for you. By working through this book it should help you to ensure that you identify what you like, dislike or what your passion is and this fits with your chosen path for the future.

Firstly, before I help you with identifying what you want in your future. I want to help you with any negative feelings that may potentially stop you moving forward and help you to cope better with the changes. Some people cope really well with change and there are others that don't. Being at school is in your comfort zone, because it is what you've done for many years. You know the environment and it is where you have your friends. Leaving school means learning about a new environment and also meeting new people and making new friends. For some of you the thought of a new environment may create fear. Being in a different environment can also lower our level of confidence.

There are different tools and techniques that can help you to regain your confidence and empower you to take on the challenge. I will share with you how you can confidently cope with change in different areas of your life.

Once you develop a negative mindset about change you will allow this to hold you back. This will result in you not being motivated to take any action and the outcome will be that you won't achieve what you want in your life. Has anyone ever explained to you about Gremlin's before? Everybody has a Gremlin. A Gremlin is that little voice in your head that provides you with self-doubt fills your head with negative thoughts and will provide you with a thousand and one excuses why you should not do something. All of the excuses your Gremlin provides you with will seem plausible at the time. Gremlins are a natural inbuilt human guilt that prevents you from exploring new environments or challenges, and are also known as the fear zone.

Gremlin's dislike you being positive and don't want you to succeed. So you must understand that your number one enemy to defeat is **YOU**. By identifying those Gremlin thoughts and replacing it with a positive mental attitude you will be able to combat negativity, otherwise you will become stuck and will not end up with the life you want.

When your Gremlin tells you something negative such as you are stupid or you will never be able to do that. I want you to look for the evidence to support what your Gremlin says. For example:

I am not stupid because...

I am capable of achieving this because...

I want you to think about what your Gremlin has said to you in the past and make a list below.

....

....

....

....

....

....

Now I want you to develop and maintain a positive mental attitude. You will need to remain positive if you are to succeed whether it is in a search for work, deciding your future career path or applying to go to university/college. A positive frame of mind will support and help you to identify opportunities. It will help you to persevere until you get on the path to the life you want. To succeed you must always look for the positive in any situation. By learning from your experiences and identifying the positive elements this will help you be one step nearer to where you want to be. So here are the three tips for you to put into practice:

1.   Be aware of the emotions and feelings you have in relation to the situation. Don't dwell on the negative feelings too much as these will hold you back. Your Gremlin will always relay negative thoughts to you. You need to change these into positives. Every negative thought that you have you must look for the evidence to support this. Negative thoughts will lead you into a deep trench or dip. I always say life is like a roller coaster. It depends how far down you go to how long it will take you to come back up the other side. When you get in the dip there is no point blaming others for where you are. Remember you are responsible for your life only you can take the action and change the situation. Everything that happens in your life is down to you and nobody else.

What can you do to uplift yourself into being positive?

What makes you happy or puts a smile on your face?

Do you have a picture of a nice scene that you can look at and imagine being there, lose yourself in the picture, and notice the detail of the picture?

Another suggestion is to read for yourself every morning the following power questions. Think about what you would say and write here:

 What are you grateful for today?..

Who do you love?...

Who loves you?...

What you are looking forward to today?.................................

What makes you happy today?...

2. A negative mindset will create a lack of confidence and low self-esteem. You may no longer feel capable or worthy of doing what you want to do. Your belief will then be that you will never get what you want. Self-belief is important if you want to change the situation you are currently in. How can you convince an employer you are right for the job if you don't believe it yourself?

Here is a list of eight positive beliefs tick the ones that you think you are:

I believe I have the ability to go to university and study.

I believe I have the confidence to fulfil all my ambitions in life.

I believe I am motivated to achieve what I want in my life.

I believe I am passionate about my hobbies.

I believe I am smart and presentable.

I believe I am honest and trustworthy.

I believe I am reliable and a good time keeper.

I believe I am friendly and approachable.

Now add a couple of your own:

You need to read these to yourself first thing in the morning and just before you go to bed at night.

3. When things don't go as planned or turn out quite right remain in a positive mindset. Ask yourself these questions:

   What have you learned from that experience to help you in the future or with your next step?

   What was the one positive thing I got from this experience?

   What could I do differently next time?

You need to allow yourself time to recover from the emotional aspect of the change and consolidate what you have already learned. Identify what you need to do to have the life you want. Believe that you can have it. Remain positive and see the change in your life as a new beginning or opportunity. Always be grateful for all the things you love that you have in your life. Sometimes we focus more on what we don't have which can cause us frustration and anxiety. Then it is difficult to recognise the opportunities that present themselves to us. To boost your confidence to take the next step, choose to take a small step which has the least risk. The reason for this is that there will be less of a fear factor and you are more likely to succeed. You can then build on your small successes. Don't forget to celebrate them this could be for example buying yourself a bar of your favourite chocolate, going to the cinema, etc.

Remember the journey and progress you make along the way is about you enjoying the journey. We can all get from A to B but never even notice the journey along the way. Living your life to the fullest means that what happens along the way of the journey is just as important. Let me give you an example of something that you may do and not really notice the experience you are having. For example:

You are going to visit a college or university. Do you notice the feeling of excitement that you have within you or are you feeling slightly nervous? What do you notice about the journey there, the places you drive through, the weather, the sounds and the people around you? What about the people you are travelling with what do you notice about them? You arrive at your destination. How are you feeling now? What do you notice about the area, the building, smell it, feel it, and live it? Close your eyes and imagine all of these things. So whatever you do along your journey in life there is always a lot to take in which is all part of the experience.

Seeking reassurance from others is alright as long as the feedback they give is positive, constructive and builds up your confidence to keep motivated. Negative people will feed your self-doubt and you will become less likely to move forward. I know in my circle of friends which one's are likely to be positive and the one's that will be negative and I regard my negative friends as dream busters. The point is, you must be very wary when you are with dream busters as they are the enemy in the future you are building. Dream busters will rob you of all your positive thoughts. If you have the inability to bounce back quickly you need to share your ideas and thoughts with your friends that are dream builders. Remember you have the recipe for success on the inside. So don't allow dream buster friends to take away your future with just one negative word, as you will struggle through life never achieving your dreams, and they will all be the first to laugh at you and call you a failure.

Write down here a list of people that you know that can impact on your life positively:

....

....

....

Making Decisions

Making decisions in your life can be extremely difficult. In your adulthood you will be making decisions on a day-to-day basis and also planning your future. You will realise there are many different choices and there is no way of knowing whether you have made the right or wrong choice. It is about making informed decisions and feeling comfortable with the reason why you made that choice. You will need to consider all your options, gather lots of information and obtain the opinions and judgement of positive people you trust. Making the wrong decision isn't that bad as you can learn from this and use this knowledge when making future decisions. Don't beat yourself up if your actions didn't quite achieve what you wanted and you start to think it was the wrong decision. Remember you made that decision based on the information that was available to you at the time. We gain most of our experience of making mistakes in our lives and learning from these. It's when we don't learn from this that we may continue to make similar mistakes. Here is a quote from Albert Einstein:

'Insanity: If you keep on doing the same over and over again and expecting different results.'

You need to view your failures as getting one step nearer to where you want to be. You view it as an experience that will help you with the next step forward.

You'll never be good enough!

Don't allow your Gremlin to start to fill your head with negative thoughts. Don't keep saying 'I should have,' or 'I could have'. Remember, what has happened is in the past and we can't re-write history but we can allow it to shape our future for the better. So then, what would you do differently next time? Use the power of a positive mindset.

To help you to make a decision about your career path or whatever you want in your future, I want you to start by completing the following activity:

Make two lists below one of your hobbies/interests and the other about what gives you a buzz or something that excites you or is really important to you...

....

....

....

....

....

....

....

....

....

....

....

....

You should have started to develop some self-awareness. Now you have identified your hobbies, interests and likes you can start to consider where they fit and how they can help to shape your future. What are the opportunities that may be open to you?

When I was sixteen I don't think I was fully aware of all the different career options that were out there. You know about the most common ones such as solicitors, doctors, nurses, etc. But there is a whole host of different jobs that help companies and organisations function with their day-to-day business. You may only be aware that a career choice exists because you know someone or may come into contact with someone that is employed in a particular job.

If you have extremely good support from your parents, friends, careers advisor you may have already reached a conclusion on this. Still working through this chapter will help you to decide whether you have made the right choice.

Now think about the following:

What would you value most in a job?

What kind of environment would you like it to have?

What would your ideal job entail?

Look at the list of words below and circle the one's you would like in your ideal job.

Working inside	Ambitious	Helping others
Working outside	Artistic	Growth
Working with machinery	Being valued	Respect
Working as part of a team	Belonging	Security
Working on own initiative	Change	Self-expression
Social activities outside of work	Communication	Status
On the job training	Competition	Support
Large corporate company	Creative	Conscientious
Small business	Friendly	Make a difference
Public sector organisation	Fun	Meeting challenges
Charitable organisation	Honesty	Learning opportunities
Intellectual stimulation		

Write some of your own here if they are not on the list:

....
....
....
....
....
....
....
....

Now you have an idea about what you like in your ideal job you now need to identify the ideal career to match this. How are you going to do that I hear you ask yourself? It is quite simple. I want you to visualise your local town and within the town there are lots of companies, shops, public sector employers, etc. They all employ people to do a variety of different jobs.

Start by drawing a diagram of your local area showing shops, offices, schools, hospitals. If you know the name of the businesses write them on. Now write down at the side of each building the jobs that people do that work within these buildings

You may need to spend some time doing some research as you may not be able to remember everything that you may see on a day-to-day basis.

Now you have your diagram carry on your research and find out the following:

What do the companies do?

What do they sell?

What do they make?

What services do they offer?

Write it down here:

....

....

....

....

....

....

....

....

....

....

....

....

Now look at the diagram and the jobs you identified and what you have now found out about the employers, what other jobs do you think they employ people for. Write them down here:

....

....

....

....

....

....

....

....

....

....

....

....

If you don't know again do some more research on the internet or ask your parents to help you.

So you now know about different employers and the types of jobs people are employed to do. Also go back to look at the activities you did on your interests, passions and values. What type of job do you think you would enjoy that would match or give you what you have already identified. Close your eyes and visualise the job/career you see yourself doing. What is it you see yourself doing?

Now write down three possible options

....

....

....

....

....

....

....

....

Research

To enable you to be sure about the decision you will make you may require some more information to help you do this. So think where you could find this information.

If you search the internet what key words do you need to use. Be clear about what it is you need to know?

Now you have gathered all your information write here your top three preferred options and the reasons for your choice?

....

....

....

....

....

....

....

Chapter 2

Is it luck or attitude?

When someone you know achieves something or is successful do you find yourself saying 'they are so lucky'. Do you really think this or is it something you just say? Now are you going to believe that you are not lucky if you don't achieve what you want or get what you want in your life? This could ultimately affect your motivation and mean that you give up at the first hurdle. So let's look at the question.

Do you think you will achieve what you want through luck or is it about attitude?

There are lots of people out there that are famous for many different reasons, whether it's for singing, inventions, sport, etc.

Do you just think they went around thinking they are lucky?

All of these people had a dream that they wanted to achieve in their life. Think about some famous people you may know such as Sir Richard Branson, Walt Disney or even your favourite footballer. You may be able to think of some others that you can relate to.

A successful outcome in anybody's life isn't about luck but through the actions taken that they may feel quite lucky. Let's consider the following definitions of luck:

Luck can be defined as an indiscriminate phenomenon of chance or fate, which one comes to increasingly appreciate less with hard work.

Also luck could be said to be something you achieved without the presence of skill.

Nothing is achieved without hard work. Firstly, you will come up with an idea and then through your thoughts you will identify the actions that are within your capability. Let me explain further, you are said to be lucky when people can see successful achievements in your life, but the visual parts of your achievements come from an idea or thought. You then take action with a positive mindset. Whatever is in your thoughts and in your attitude helps you to create the right environment to get a positive outcome.

When you are positive you will walk around with your head held high and be able to see the opportunities around you. If you have a negative mindset you will be walking around with your head down and not see the opportunities. You will miss opportunities.

Take for instance, your clothes, shoes, car, house etc., they were all invented and created by someone who did put their mind to work and followed the principle of creation. If you learn to understand that the mind is capable of creating ideas combined with the right atmosphere it is more likely to work out, no matter what your dreams or goals are. There are people who were the first to discover some things but others have then built on this. The question is not about how hard it is to achieve the idea, but how willingly ready are you paying the price of making that idea work, through being positive and consistent persistent actions? In a nutshell, success could be rightly defined as, preparation meets opportunity.

Write down some names here of famous people you know and what they have achieved

....
....
....
....
....
....

So, how did these people get their dreams to come true?

What did they do to make it happen?

Do you perceive them to be lucky to be where they are today?

How do you think they managed to achieve what they have today?

Do you think they found what they wanted easily or through hard work to achieve their successes?

To achieve what they wanted in life they would have had to be motivated, have determination and most of all energy. It is very important to maintain your energy levels as this will maintain your positive thoughts. It will take you through the rough patches and help you to keep on going no matter what happens.

Here are some examples of famous people of what they did and the results they got of being motivated until they got the result they wanted.

Did you know that Walt Disney used to be a journalist who was told he wasn't creative? Everything that Disney created has been extremely creative. It has enabled him to create a kingdom of fantasy for both the young and old.

Edison invented the light bulb. He was turned down thousands of times but he had believed and knew he had a good invention. He saw every failure as being one step nearer to success. He never gave up.

As you can see success doesn't come easy as you have to always be taking that small step to get you one step nearer. It is important to not take on board negative comments that people may make. This could result in shattering your dream as the self-doubt will start to creep in. You need to keep on believing in yourself and what it is you want to achieve.

Achieving your success isn't about being lucky but about being focused. Now, imagine for one moment your life is like a car. If you didn't have a steering wheel how would you get it to go where you wanted it to be. So having a focus for your life enables you to steer your life in the right direction. People that are focused know what they are looking for and when opportunities present themselves you are more likely to see them. So, it isn't about luck but it is about positioning yourself in the right places where the opportunities are more likely to present themselves to you.

I also mentioned earlier about attitude. What attitude do you think people have to enable them to be successful?

Here are some of the attributes I think successful people have:

- Determination
- Perseverance
- Focused
- Motivated
- Full of Energy
- Passionate
- Self-Belief
- Confidence
- Good Communications
- Masters of Time
- Trusts Intuition
- Action Orientated
- Good Listener

Looking at the above attributes take a few minutes to recognise the ones you think you have and the ones you need to develop.

To be able to achieve anything you need to maintain a positive mindset. The minute you have negative thoughts or you allow your Gremlin to creep in, you will lose the ability to move forward and not see the opportunities available to you. Don't blame others if things don't work out or look at others with envy of what they have. Those people will have been focused and will have seen the opportunities. They will have taken lots of action to get them what they have. So don't allow yourself to become negative. Blaming others is a drain too and a negative view, this won't get you anywhere. Take responsibility for your own actions and the results you get. If things don't work out, look at what you are doing. Here is a quote from Albert Einstein:

'A person who never made a mistake never tried anything new'.

So re-assess what you are doing, make changes to what you do to ensure you are successful and get the results that you want. You can learn from your mistakes which will enable you to do it differently the next time or come up with a new idea.

A positive mindset is about being motivated, having the passion about what you want, perseverance and taking action. All of these combined will keep you moving nearer and nearer to your goal.

You will get many knock backs along the way but stay positive. You need to keep on bouncing back. Pick yourself back up and dust yourself down. Remember when you give up and stop taking action you are out of the game. Remain confident and strong.

Let me give you an example about how to positively deal with failure:

When you don't get the job you were interviewed for, look at this as it is one step nearer to getting the job for you. See it as a practice interview. Then ask for feedback. You are now aware where you can improve for the next interview. Then practice this and this will enable you to make the changes to improve for the next time.

Something else you could do is to define your success. So, for example if you were going for a job interview you could decide what would make it a successful interview for you. This doesn't have to be about getting the job but could be about answering all the questions confidently.

So now you understand that it isn't about luck and more about your frame of mind and positive mental attitude move on to the next chapter.

Chapter 3

Self-Belief

In the previous chapter we talked about luck and positive mental attitude. This briefly mentioned about you being focused. Without a focus you will not achieve anything. In this chapter we are going to look at what you are focused on and your self-belief in relation to this. We also previously looked at self-belief in the first chapter of this book so you can now build on this here.

So let me tell you about a young man that I worked with. His name was Daniel he is extremely focused on what he wants. Daniel knows what he wants and when he wants to achieve it by. He identifies the actions he needs to take to achieve his goal. Every action he takes moves him one step nearer to where he wants to be. He has a passion for what he wants to achieve and this is the main driver that keeps him focused and motivated. Without that feeling of passion he would find it difficult to stay focused and motivated on what he wants in his life. Daniel has a vision of his goal which focuses him on how it will feel when he has achieved it. Daniel needs to be able to live his dream. Daniel also has self-belief that he can achieve his dream. Daniel tells himself every day that he can achieve his goal. This maintains a positive mind set and gives him confidence to continue to take action. When I speak to him he always uses positive language, for example whenever I ask him about his goal he always responds with positive statements such as 'when I achieve my goal'. Not 'if ' I ever achieve my goal. This is because he has a very strong belief.

Do you use positive or negative language when you speak?

Negative phrases I have heard clients say are:

'I will try'

'I probably will'

Do you use positive language in relation to what you want in your life?

Start to notice when you talk what words you do use.

Here is a list of phrases. Tick the one's that you say:

'I will try'   'If I ever achieve...'

'I am going to...'   'But...'

'I will...'   'But and...'

'I probably will'   Add some of your own:

'May be I will'   ....

'I possibly could'   ....

'When I achieve...'   ....

Now look at the phrases you have ticked are these negative or positive. If there are some negative words consider how you could change these to a positive and read it out aloud.

You have to believe you can have what you want. The only way to do this is to use language that shows that you believe that it will happen and you will have the things you want in your life. Remember change your words and you will change your life. Self-belief has to come from within you; nobody else can do this for you.

When focusing on something new you want in your life, it can create an element of fear, excitement or even anxiety. The reason for this is that your future is an area of uncertainty. Moving on to greener pastures means stepping outside of your comfort zone. Being in your comfort zone means it is safe and you feel a sense of security. Let me explain about the three different zones, we can all go in and out of, depending on what it is we are pursuing in our life.

There are a number of things I know have made me at some point or another dip in and out of these zones. For example, when I was setting up my business, this used to take me into my panic zone as this was unfamiliar territory for me. If I delivered a new training session I had written then I may be in my stretch zone as this was challenging me in a new area of knowledge and skill. My comfort zone would be doing all the things that I always do without even giving it a second thought.

So let's take a look at the three different zones. See if you can recognise what fits in each for you and write them in the space provided.

Comfort Zone

This is the zone where everything you do is within your capabilities you can do it easily and it may not particularly challenge you. It is something that you know or an environment that you know. For example:

You can't swim so you decide to stay on land and not get into the small boat. You are now staying in your comfort zone where there is no fear or panic.

For you this may be School, riding a bike, a particular subject at school that you are good at.

....

....

....

....

Stretch Zone

Is where you feel a slight element of fear and excitement about doing something new and different in your life? It may mean learning new knowledge and skills or taking you to a new environment. For example:

You can't swim and you are put into the small boat in the middle of the lake with a life jacket on. You still feel some fear but you know that you can't drown as you have a life jacket. This would put you in your stretch zone.

For you this may be learning something new, meeting new people.

....

....

....

....

Panic Zone

Now this is the zone that will cause you extreme anxiety. In this state you may find it impossible to move forward. For example:

You can't swim and you are put in the middle of a lake in a small boat. The level of fear may be so great that the thought of doing this makes you feel anxious. You would be in your panic zone.

For you this may be doing a presentation, performing

....
....
....
....

So, what could help you, to step outside your comfort zone?   Here are some examples:

Singing a song solo may be in your panic zone but singing with other people would take you into your stretch zone.

Sitting in your exams may take you into your panic zone but doing lots of revision may take you into your stretch zone.

Going to the cinema on your own may take you to your stretch zone but meeting your friends outside the cinema would put you in your comfort zone.

Take a few minutes to think about a situation where it would make you feel out of your comfort zone and what you would need to do to make you feel more comfortable about it. Write your thoughts here:

....
....

....

....

....

....

....

Here are some suggestions that can help you when outside of your comfort zone;

- Accept the change by making a definite decision to do something different about your present situation.

- Take control of the situation by creating a plan this will give you a clear focus.

- Maintain a positive attitude by doing something positive every day, no matter how small, that will help you to get your end result. Remember the right action takes you one step nearer to where you want to be.

- Accept that sometimes you are going to fail but not trying is more of a failure. But the difference is that attempted failures give you a clue on how it could be done in a different way, so in a real sense attempted failures are part of every invention of humankind.

- Believe that what you are doing is important and make it a priority

- Looking into the future sometimes will bring on thoughts that create fear and panic, so focus mainly on the here and now.

- Don't let opportunities pass you by.

So now you have recognised what can help you move from your comfort zone. We now need to work on your self-belief because without this you won't achieve anything.

Why is self-belief so important?

Self-belief is important because:

You will recognise the abilities and talent you have to be able to succeed in achieving your goal. This will help you to develop and strengthen your courage.

Always welcome self doubt with a ready mind set of positivity because every time you remind yourself about your strength and skills when faced with a drowning thought of negativity, you develop more courage that is necessary to keep you moving.

It helps to maintain your confidence.

It drives you forward.

If you have no self belief you will not be able to imagine how it will feel when you have achieved what you want in your life. When you were a small child you probably had lots of imagination. Remember how you used to be able to play make believe, we used to be able to pretend we were somewhere else, doing something different and were creative with what we were doing and saying. As we get older we allow our knowledge of past experiences to shape our view and opinions in life, which can stop us moving forward. So let your thoughts and feelings flow spontaneously.

Refer back to the positive beliefs you ticked in Chapter 1. Can you add any more to this list. Write them here:

1.

2.

3.

Make sure you read your positive beliefs first thing in a morning and just before you go to sleep on a night. Going to sleep with positive thoughts will always make you feel better and allow you to meditate whilst asleep and first thing in a morning allows you to have positive thoughts at the beginning of each day. The more you read them the more you will believe the statements you wrote which will enable you to believe in yourself.

I just want to give you something else to think about. The more positive your mind set is the more likely your day will go well. If things don't go as well as expected, try to find some learning from this. If you can't shake off the day then start again tomorrow. The fact is if you are in a positive frame of mind things that don't go to plan doesn't always feel quite as bad as when you are in a negative frame of mind. A positive frame of mind enables you to see things in a more positive light. You will also bounce back quicker and cope better with anything that goes wrong.

So by reading your positive beliefs every morning this will maintain positive expectations for the day.

Chapter 4

Clarifying and Setting Your Goals

From the previous chapters you have now decided what you want in life to be able to clearly define your goal.

Do you now know what you want in your life?

Have you now got a clear focus?

Remember you are more likely to get what you want in life if you are positive and have self-belief. We have already looked at having a clear focus and also about having that self-belief to help you to move towards getting what you want. Hopefully by now you have made a decision about what it is that you do want. All you need is to have that passion and really want it enough because life will definitely test you to know how seriously you do want it.

Write down here what it is that makes you have a buzz or get excited about what you want in your life and give it a score from 1 – 10. Ten being extremely excited and one being no passion...

Interesting   *Challenging*

Fun   *Learning new skills*

Enables you to meet people   *Helping others*

Step nearer to your future   *Competitive*

Sense of belonging   *Sense of purpose*

Being creative   *Builds confidence*

List some of your own here...

...

...

Setting goals for your future is really important. You need to be very clear about what it is you want and when you want to achieve it. This means that you have to break your goals into achievable objectives with definite dates. If you don't give your goal a date it will just be a dream. You need a specific date to work with. So let's have a look at writing down what you want in the short term (one year objectives) and then the long term (one year to five year objectives). This is very important because it helps you to monitor your progress and you can learn to improve on your technicality on how to go about handling your next objective.

Now write them down in the boxes below in a simple way that you can understand:

Short Term (one year)
Long Term (one-five years)

Here are some top tips on how to write your goals:

- Always begin with the end in mind

- Have a clear understanding of your destination

- Know where you are going

- What is it you want to achieve

- Understand where you are now

- Ensure the steps that you take are in the right direction

- You can tackle anything tangible that you want to change or improve in your life

- If there is a long list decide on the priorities, because you can't achieve everything at once

- Properly set goals that will be motivating and build up confidence

- Firstly set a larger scale goal, then break these down into smaller and smaller targets that you must achieve to reach your overall goal

- Goals must be positive

- Write the goal down

Goals should be written as a SMART goal. SMART stands for:

Specific

Measurable

Appealing

Realistic

Time bound

Specific – Your goal must be specific, so specify what you want to achieve. For example saying you want to 'get fitter' isn't enough as your brain does not have a clear way to interpret that type of instruction. Fitness for you may be getting slimmer, being more energetic, getting more toned, growing stronger or perhaps all of the above.

Measurable – You need to be able to measure whether you are achieving your goal or not. If for example you wanted to tackle your smoking habit you must quantify what you want to achieve. This may be to cut out smoking completely from your life or to reduce the number of cigarettes you smoke as a stated amount. Again your brain needs a clear instruction or it doesn't know where to start, and procrastination sets in.

Achievable/Appealing – It may be achievable because other people have done it already but you are not other people. Sometimes thinking about this as a measure can sometimes get in your way. For example think of Roger Bannister running a mile in 4 minutes – if he had applied the achievable measure he may never have attempted to set this record as the whole world was telling him it was impossible.

The goal must be appealing to you. The focus needs to be put on the continuation on the current path and the long term effects this will have. Identify the negative associations of not making any change and then the positive of how your life could be once the change has been achieved. Focus on how much you would enjoy the changes in your life. If you don't find the goal appealing you can't get anywhere with it because the goal doesn't motivate you. Either make the goal appealing or find a goal that does motivate you.

Realistic – External measures of what may be achievable, such as comparing your circumstances with those of others, may not be very helpful to you. However, you must still ensure that the goal is realistic for you, in both the current circumstances of your life and current level of ability. You can have a very challenging and stretching goal that takes you out of your comfort zone, but you need to ensure that it sets you up for your own success. Take into account any constraints as this may mean you have to take a longer journey or slightly adjust your plans. Also consider can you realistically achieve your goal with the resources that you have. Being realistic doesn't mean you have to set limits for yourself but you need to work out how to walk before you can run.

Time-bound – When do you want to achieve your goal by? Give it a specific deadline to achieve it by or you may find you may never achieve it. Set timed milestones to help you succeed in getting you to the point where you want to be. You can take small steps to help you move closer. The times can be adjusted as you complete one milestone you may find that there is something else that needs to be done before completing the next milestone. Having timed milestones helps you to focus on the deadlines that are right for you. Also having a time bound goal is one of the best ways to stop procrastination.

Here is an example of how to write your goal:

By 30 September 2013 I want to be employed as a Graphic Designer in a large organisation working as part of a team. I will be earning £23,000 with pension and 25 days holiday. I will feel happy, challenged and content in my work.

I will have achieved my BA (honors) degree in Social Work by 31 May 2014.

Now write your goal here:

....

....

....

....

....

....

....

....

So now you have your goals close your eyes and visualise what you want in your life. Imagine you have achieved your goal and what is happening. Imagine how you feel and what your friends or family are saying to you. The feeling and emotion you get from this visualisation can help you to maintain your motivation when you start to have doubts or things don't quite go to plan.

If you ever have any negative thoughts or images about you achieving your goal think about how you could change these. Remember the chapter on self-belief. You need to believe you can have what you want in your life.

The way I maintain my positive mind set is every day I think about all the things I am grateful for. By concentrating on what I have and not focusing on what I don't have. This keeps you in a place of being happy and positive. How many times do you hear yourself saying 'I wish I had...' but what about all the things that you do have already. To put it in perspective there are people in the world that don't have much in their life but they are still happy and grateful for what they have. We can go through life not taking notice of our environment. Cape Verde is a place where I feel at peace and where I chose to write this book. When in Cape Verde I decided to take notice of the environment. I noticed the sound of the sea, the fragrant aroma in the air, the heat, the colours of the flowers, palm trees and the sea. So think about your environment, what is there that you can be grateful for. Start today and be grateful for what you already have.

Write a list today of ten things that you are grateful for.

1.

2.

3.

3.

5.

6.

7.

8.

9.

10.

Gratefulness   vs.   *Ungratefulness*

You could buy yourself a nice notebook that you can continue to write ten things every day if that helps you to maintain a positive mindset. Try it, you will see that it does work.

Chapter 5

Motivation

Motivation is of vital importance if you are to achieve anything that you want. As motivation is a driving force, without this you are going nowhere.

To be motivated you have to have an understanding about your motives and then be able to satisfy your needs. Do you know what your needs are?

These can be socio-psychological needs for example:

Feedback, honesty, feeling of belonging, responsibility, credibility

Or even intellectual needs, e.g. interesting, self-fulfilment, challenges. Material incentives could be another.

So let's take a look at what we mean by motivation.

There are two different elements of motivation they are intrinsic and extrinsic.

Intrinsic motivation is about the internal rewards that you get from moving towards your goals. This is about the enjoyment and the fun from taking the action and the fulfilment it gives you. It is a challenge and a sense of achievement. Each step you take that gets you one step nearer gives you the encouragement for you to continue. The rewards you give yourself to celebrate your successes are also internal.

Extrinsic motivation can be less effective as the rewards come from outside of you from external sources. These can be such things as praise from your parents or extra pocket money for doing well. With extrinsic motivation you are dependent on other people. If this does not happen then potentially there is an extreme possibility that you may lose interest.

Without either intrinsic or extrinsic motivation you will not achieve anything. Which one would motivate you more intrinsic or extrinsic?

Motivation is also about having a positive mindset. Once you have a negative mindset about achieving your goal you are less likely to move forward. Your negative mindset may be caused through your fears or even your lack of self-belief. Going on your journey you are going to get set-backs. With a positive mind set you will pick yourself up dust yourself down and keep on going.

So now that you have your goal you need to get yourself motivated. Remember everything I have asked you to do in this book plays a part in you being successful in getting what you want. This is the reason you were asked to identify your passion. Passion can become your key motivator. If you have a burning desire to achieve something you will be more likely to remain motivated.

What motivates you?

When you have been motivated in the past doing something, what was happening then?

Take a minute to write this down here:

....

....

....

....

....

Everyone is different so what motivates one person may not be the same for another. You may be motivated as you want to show your parents what you can achieve, it may give you some sense of achievement, you may have something to prove to others, you like a challenge or once you have a pathway to your career you are on your way to having all the other things you want in your life e.g. holidays, car, house, etc.

You just need to have some self-awareness of what it is that motivates you.

As time goes on and you get weary your motivation can dwindle. You may feel that you are not making any progress or achieving anything.

Do you start to wonder what the point is?

Do you feel like you are not achieving anything?

These negative thoughts are what will make you become de-motivated. It is so easy to focus on what you haven't got rather than what you have. To be motivated you need to want it enough to be able to pursue it. If you don't you need to re-assess what you think you want as you need to have the passion and drive that will keep you motivated. So re-visit your goal and look at what you need to do to change it to give you that passion and drive to take it forward. If you stop taking action you will take yourself out of the game. By not taking any action nothing will change and you won't move forward. I will talk about action more in the next chapter.

On a scale of 1 – 10 how motivated are you feeling right now to take action to identify what you want that will give you a clearer direction to your future. One being poor, ten being extremely good. Circle where you think you are

| 1 | 2 | 3 | 4 | 5 | 6 | 7 | 8 | 9 | 10 |

So how can you maintain your motivation through the difficult times? Here are some useful tips for you to use to help you to do this:

1. Make sure you have a clear focus for what you want to achieve. Imagine that you have that dream job or whatever you want in your life. When you think about it how **do you feel**? Do you feel excited, happy, etc. This will give you that feel good factor. Seek out the opportunities to being one step nearer.

2. Keep a success diary. Complete it everyday with one thing that you have achieved this will give you a feel good factor. It doesn't matter how big or small that achievement is. When you are having a down day read your successes. This will bring back your positive frame of mind. Sometimes you start to think you haven't achieved anything or moved any nearer to where you want to be. Your diary will help you remember.

3. Perseverance is key to achieving what you want. Remember to never give up. If you don't succeed don't view this as failure, see this as you are one step nearer to you getting what you want. If one thing doesn't work out then what else could you do? Try something different.

Chapter 6

Taking Action

If you are to achieve what you want in life you need to have determination and the hard work will almost certainly pay off. But remember you have to take the right action to get the results you want. If you are not seeing any results take some time to think about the actions you are doing and what actions you could do that would get the results.

How good are you at managing your time?

Do you tend to think I can do that tomorrow?

Do you tend to get distracted by your friends or find playing a computer game more important?

Every minute you lie in bed until lunchtime you have lost half the day when you could be taking action. Every minute you sit watching television or playing on your computer again is wasted time. Let this be your reward for getting the actions done that will help you achieve what you want to achieve.

How you effectively manage time is important as suddenly you find that weeks and months have passed and nothing has happened or changed. The more time we have the more we seem to waste time unless we stay focused you will just drift along.

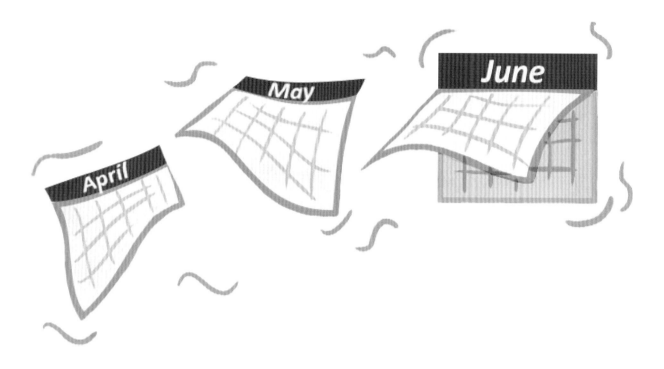

What could you do to help you to do this?

To manage your time effectively you need to be focused on the key tasks you need to undertake that day. The sooner you get them done the more time you will have to reward yourself by doing something enjoyable. I always write lists of what I need doing each day and cross them off as I do them this gives me a sense of achievement and satisfaction. Having a list of tasks though can sometimes overwhelm you so to stop this happening I use my diary to block out time for what I need to do. I always do the one thing I least want to do first. Once you have done this everything else on your list will seem easy to do. Otherwise what happens is you do the easy tasks or things you like doing first over the one you don't want to do. Then you decide you haven't the time to do the task you least want to do so there it remains on the list. It then gets moved to another day and there is the risk that you keep moving it down and it never gets done. There are many other things you could do to manage your time. Think about what would work well for you.

Friends and family are very good at being a distraction. They will ask you to do things like chores, look after a younger sibling or go places. You will need to become assertive.

What do I mean by being assertive?

Being assertive means about being able to think for yourself, speak out and stand your ground in personal, social and career situations. Being assertive is a choice of behaviour and it is about respecting yourself and the people you have to deal with in different situations.

Assertive means that you acknowledge that you are in charge of your actions, your choices and your life. Part of being assertive is about learning how to say 'no'. Friends or family may ask you to do something and you may already have decided that you are doing something else that day. What you had planned to do may be the time that you have set aside to work on your future. Being able to say 'no' will be key to you moving closer to you being successful.

From time to time we all come up with excuses as to why we can't do something. Sometimes we can use what other people want as a distraction as we are putting off doing the action that will move us nearer to our goals. You may find that playing a computer game suddenly seems quite important and then before you know it you have no time left in the day. You will find yourself saying 'I will do it tomorrow'. Tomorrow will come and you may find something else more important.

Whenever my daughter had an assignment to write for school/university she would put it off. Her distraction was cleaning and tidying her bedroom. Suddenly this task seemed to be extremely important even though it had been needed for some time. She would then start her assignment when she had finished by which time she had lost half a day. You should prioritise what you need to do that is important and do this first thing. In my daughter's case the deadline for the assignment was more important as the untidy bedroom would still be there when she finished her assignment. Cleaning the bedroom did not achieve her objectives. So stop and think for a moment what your priorities are?

Putting actions off for the next day will not move you forward. What I have learned in life is that unexpected things can happen which are circumstances that are out of our control. So ensure you allow plenty of time to take the actions so they are not last minute. Imagine if you had a job application for a few weeks and you think I will do that the day before it needs to be in and guess what your printer jams. This will cause you to become stressed and will cause you more work as you then have to find some other way of printing it. From time to time there will be circumstances that arise when you can't do what you planned for example you may get a phone call that asks if you can go for a job interview that day. But if you are leaving plenty of time you can just re-schedule what you need to do for the next day.

Do you tend to leave things to the last minute?

Having lots of time on your hands can mean you constantly put off doing the actions that will achieve what you want in your life. Try to get some structure or routine to your day. You may be someone that works best under pressure. This can be difficult when you suddenly find yourself with no pressure from anyone other than what you know you need to do. You may have lots of things you need to do and this can make you feel quite overwhelmed. So break this down into baby steps.

Firstly, you need to decide on what actions you need to take.

Write here a list of all the things you need to do to help you achieve your goal

....

....

....

....

....

....

....

....

....

....

What you have to remember is if you want something to change then you have to take action. What you have in your life is down to you.

Having some structure to your day is vital as soon as possible. It needs to be a combination of actions towards your goal and leisure. We can all make excuses for not doing something as you have been 'busy'. Busy doing what? You may have been busy but probably not doing the actions to achieve your goal. Another excuse 'I didn't have time', you need to make time and only you alone can do that.

How many excuses have you made so far?

Here are is a list of excuses that may have stopped you so far from taking action tick the one's you use or write down one of your own:

I haven't had time

I'll do it tomorrow

I'll just play on my games for half an hour

My friends wanted me to go out with them

My friends needed me to help them

I have got a lot of homework

I had to look after my younger brother/sister

I am too tired

I'll just watch my favourite television programme

....

....

Your excuse might start by doing something else for an hour and before you know it the whole evening, day or weekend has gone and still hasn't been done. So make sure you are busy doing the things that make progress to what you want to achieve.

How could you structure your days to achieve what you want?

Here are some suggestions to help you get started:

1.   You need to view your work now as taking actions to move you to your future. Research needs to be systematic so prepare a list of all the places you can find information to help you move forward. Allow between 2-3 hours each week to work on the actions towards your goals. Remember the effort you put into this will move you closer to the result you want.

2. Talking or meeting friends are important as the more people you tell about your goals for the future the more people you have supporting you and finding information on your behalf. This will be fun catching up with people that you haven't seen for ages.

3.   Having some form of exercise is important too as this will keep you fit, de-stress and build up your endorphins. It will make you feel better in yourself. Exercise can be free for example: walking, running or cycling.

4.   Make a list of all the things you have never got round to doing and plan these into your spare time. This will give you a sense of achievement.

5.   Use a diary or the calendar on the computer to plan in the time to do the above tasks.

6.   Remember your days or weeks need to have a mixture of leisure and social activities to retain an element of fun in your life.

7. Are you still finding that you are making excuses that you haven't had time?

So what is really happening?

Does the job seem bigger than it actually is?

Is it not interesting enough or is it something you don't like doing?

You think it's not urgent so you can leave it to another day?

Other things are more important?

Or are you still easily distracted?

Before you know it, a week, a month and then a year has past. Just where has the time gone. You look back at what you have achieved, where you are now and where you wanted to be. You might even think if only you had been more organised. At school you have a structured day you know what time you have to get up, when you start and finish. Then you make time for your friends, hobbies and interests.

So, what is it that stops you from taking action now?

Tick the one's that stop you or write one of your own here:

- Don't like talking to people you don't know

- Lack of confidence

- Don't know where to find out about something

- Don't know where to start

- Fear

- Lack of motivation

- What if...

....

....

....

All of these things are what we call barriers. For some reason we find barriers that stop us taking action. These tend to be perceived barriers that seem real to you at the time. Let's have a look at some of the things you may have identified. You may have some others but these are the most common one's that people go through. So let's go through these one by one and have a look at what you can do to overcome these.

Lack of Confidence

Lacking in confidence can be the biggest barrier to stopping you taking action. That self-doubt will have crept in again; your Gremlin will be filling your head with negative self-talk. You will be able to build up your confidence by doing small actions that take you out of your comfort zone. So do something that you have never done before. Also you can sit in front of a mirror every day and tell yourself 'I am confident and strong'. Each time check out your body language and see how you are

portraying your confidence to others. Continue reading your positive beliefs that you wrote out in a previous chapter. This will also help to drive you forward with what you need to do.

Don't know where to find information

This can be a big problem in moving forward but sometimes we know the answer ourselves but we just can't see it. The internet is very useful for finding out information or even your local library. Other people are also a great source of information so talk to lots of people this may be your friends, relatives, school teacher, etc. Don't be scared to ask. If you don't ask the question you will never know what knowledge other people have that can help you on your way to being successful.

Don't know where to start

Sometimes you can be so overwhelmed by the bigger picture it can be difficult to make a start and decide what to do first. Break it down into smaller bite size chunks. Then write a list of what you think you need to do and then prioritise these into an order of importance. Decide when you are going to do them and give yourself a deadline for doing them. Remember if you don't give yourself a deadline you may never get started.

Fear

Looking into the future sometimes will bring on thoughts that create fear and panic, so focus mainly on the present. When we allow the fear and panic to come into our head, it will cause negative thoughts. You may start to look at the reasons why you can't have what you want; you may look at all the things that could happen. For example Sarah was offered a job but in the end she didn't accept it. The reason for this was because she thought about all of the things that could potentially happen. She brought into this her previous life experiences and assumed the same would happen in this employment. Instead what she could have done was accepted the job and decided to see how it went in the first six months and then make a decision whether it was the job for her. Whilst she was in a job it is far easier to find another than when you are not in one, because employers see you as being more employable.

Did you know **FEAR** could stand for?

F alse

E vidence

A ppearing

R eal

Lack of Motivation

We looked at motivation in Chapter 5. So if this is what you are struggling with re-visit this chapter and work through the exercises again to identify the reason why you are not motivated. We can all at some time or another become de-motivated. There are many reasons for this you could feel drained and tired or you may have been unwell. All of these factors can cloud the way you feel and make it difficult to move forward.

When you come up against barriers like these ask yourself this question 'what do you need to do to help you to overcome it'. You usually know what the answer is yourself you just need to take time out to think about what it is that will help you. Think about what is happening and how you are feeling.

What if...

This is similar to fear. You start to come up with millions of reasons or excuses of things that might happen. What if this happens? What if that happens? Again this is about looking ahead. Nobody knows what could happen in the future, so there is no point in imagining what could potentially happen. Just stay in the here and now, the present day. Take action and face any issues when they arise but don't try and identify them before they happen. What if... can also be a positive. If you try something and it doesn't work out you could say 'What if I try this opportunity?'

Here is a useful technique to help you solve a problem and to manage the fear about a situation. So start by imagining all the negative 'what if's. Here is an example:

You go to an exam and you look at the paper and see only two questions you can answer. You will start to panic and wonder what you can do in that situation. Here are some options:

1. You can do the questions that you can answer.

2. Write a spider diagram to find out how much you know about one of the other questions.

3. Write what you can.

4. If you fail you can take the exam again.

All of these will start to take the fear out of failure.

Chapter 7

Perseverance

Do you ever feel like just giving up and walking away from it?

Has your confidence level started to dip?

Do you have self-doubt as to whether you have the ability?

In this chapter it is about you understanding the importance of perseverance. Perseverance is about commitment to yourself to do whatever is necessary to achieve what you want in your life. Perseverance is about you not giving up even though you may be faced with difficulties and in spite that others may tell you that what you want you may never achieve. To achieve something that is easy is something that anyone can do. The harder it is the more of an achievement it is for you.

If you read about successful peoples' words such as 'persistence', 'perseverance', 'tenacity', stickability are used to describe them. These are personality traits that we have to develop if we want to be successful in life. With these traits you will be able to overcome the challenges you may be faced with.

How many of you have learned how to swim or ride a bike? That was through 'perseverance' and 'stick ability'. Otherwise you would have given up at the first hurdle. You were probably given encouragement by your parents too. So remember you can still have that perseverance now as the people that achieve the most are the one's that keep on going through the challenges that reap the most rewards.

So now you have decided what you want in your life you now need to learn how to keep going and what you have achieved to need to learn how to keep it.

What do I mean by that?

I mean that you must never lose sight of what made you choose what you wanted right now. Remember there was a reason why you chose what you have in your life. Sometimes when things aren't going quite to plan it is easy to forget why we chose the path we are on.

So, write down here the reason behind your choice or decision:

....

....

....

....

....

Was your choice about your passion or a stepping stone to where you want to be in the future? It could even be something you are doing in the interim until you make a decision about what you really want to do or make headway with your future.

Sometimes things can be quite tough and challenging and this can take you out of your comfort zone.

Well don't despair. We all go through this when we are out of our comfort zone. You need to persevere and build back up your enthusiasm. Sometimes it is easier to walk away from something rather than have perseverance and work through it. Whenever I started a new job the first six months were always hard. As I had to settle in to a new environment, meet new people, learn all about the job I was doing and what other people were doing. In the first two months I sometimes had thoughts as to whether the job was for me, but because I persevered I got past this stage and usually found that I really liked the job. I found I felt like this because it was all new and I was constantly learning to improve my new self confidence in that environment. Every organisation I've worked for did things differently and I had to adapt to the change. Sometimes I found this easier than others.

If you are starting to feel that you are going to give up then let's try and identify what may be causing you to want to do this.

What has happened to make you feel this way?

Write down here what you have identified:

✏️ ....

....

....

....

....

So now you have identified what the cause is you now need to work on the solution.

Take some time to think about what you can do to regain enthusiasm or enable you to persevere.

Write down here what you could do to help you persevere:

✏️ ....

....

....

....

....

....

....

Here are some of my top tips to help you persevere through the tough times:

1. When the going gets tough remind yourself of the reason why you are on the path you have chosen.

2. Maintain a Positive Mindset. You will achieve what you want to achieve you just need to keep going.

3. Don't Give Up! Don't allow others to stop you working towards your goal. Someone or something may offer you an excuse to give up, say "NO." So many people are not living their lives to the full potential as they have allowed someone or something to steal their dreams.

4. Overcome Fear. Do not allow fear to stop you moving forward and dictate who you are or what you are able to accomplish.

5. Believe in Yourself; remember you have a plan for your life and opportunities will present themselves at the right time. You need to be ready to take up these opportunities to fulfil your dream.

6. Learn from Your Failures. You will experience failures along the way. There is a reason for this. They will make you a stronger person and contribute towards your development as a person.

7. Welcome Difficult Times as they make us stronger and more resilient. Through difficult times focus on what you have and not on what you have lost. Move on from seeing the problem and search for opportunities that may exist as a result of the situation. Focus on how it may have helped you learn about your purpose in life and how it has made your life more meaningful.

8. Be Totally Committed to Your Goals. You need to be committed 100%. You need to invest your time and self into what you want to achieve. Extraordinary success demands extraordinary commitment.

9. Always Do Your Best. Less than your best will not do.

10. Meet the Challenge. You will need to be disciplined, work hard, but taking the required action to meet the challenge is what it takes to succeed. There are no short cuts, no side steps, and no cheating.

11. Never Ever Give Up.

Note: Never lose sight of what you want to achieve and always be grateful for what you have now.

Chapter 8

How to Improve Your Employability

In this chapter I want to help you to improve your employability. By improving your employability you are more likely to be employed and also sustain yourself within employment once you have got that job. You will recognise what employers are looking for and be able to evidence to employers that you have what they want. Getting that all important job interview is key. This can get you in front of an employer allowing them to find out more about you as a person. Of course you can find out more about the company and the person you would be working for as well.

So what do employers want?

Here are the important skills and abilities for getting, keeping and improving a job.

As an employee you should be:

- Honest

- Dependable

- Reliable

- Punctual

- Gets along well with other people

- Accepts and handle responsibility

- Cooperates with supervisors and be flexible

- Willing to undertake further job skills training

- Speaks well and listen effectively

- Works with minimum supervision

- Ability to solve problems

- Demonstrates relevant job skills

As an employee you may have all of the above but the most important thing of all is to have the right attitude so this is more important than skills. You would require the right attitude in the following:

- Motivation

- Enthusiasm

- Team Working

- Communication

- Flexibility

- Adaptability

- Initiative

- Ongoing development

How do you think that you fit that list?

Are there any areas you think you may be weak in or could improve?

Write down here which areas you may need to improve and how you are going to do this:

....

....

....

....

....

To get yourself into a job you need to understand the recruitment process so let me start to explain this to you here. Once you understand this you will know how to write your job applications/Curriculum Vitae to meet the requirements of the job and what the employer is looking for. The process in the relevant order is as follows:

- Job Advert

- Application Pack (Information/Job Description/Person Specification)

- Short listing

- An invitation to interview

- Interviews

- Job Offer

Job Advert

This is just the start of the process. The advert will clearly define the job and the type of person the company is looking for. It will provide contact details to enable you to obtain more information. If you are interested but not sure whether you have the right qualification request the information anyway. This will give you an idea of what you may need in the area of personal development. You could also submit an application to see what happens as it does depend on the standard of the applicants at the time, so don't totally dismiss it. Some adverts may just give you a brief outline of the job and request that you submit a Curriculum Vitae (CV). In this instance make sure you change your CV so it matches the job role you are applying for. If there isn't a lot of information then search on the internet for a similar job and find out what the requirements are.

Application Pack

The information or application pack should provide you with details of the job, a job description and a person specification. The job description will identify the key tasks of the job role. The person specification informs you of what they are looking for in the person they want to recruit. So for example: excellent communication skills.

In your job application you would need to demonstrate each point on the person specification. So for example with communication skills you could write the following:

I have good communication skills both verbally and written. I can communicate with customers on the telephone. I have the ability to communicate in written format by email or when writing letters.

If you don't demonstrate each point and provide examples you are less likely to get an interview. Getting the interview is what you want. Try and structure your application in relation to the layout of the person specification as it makes it easier for the employer when they are short listing to find all the relevant information. You have to realise if an employer has one hundred and fifty applicants they will skim read each application to find the information they require. So make it easy for them.

Short listing

In the short listing process if followed true to form a scoring sheet will be used where it is identified for each applicant what elements of the criteria they have met. The employer may decide how many applicants they want to interview so for example if they want eight and there are ten suitable candidates the application forms would have to be re-visited to see who out of those ten are the most suitable of the applicants. This could be through experience, knowledge, skills, etc., or even how you have come across in your application as there may be something about you that they really like and want to find out more about you.

An invitation to interview

Letters will be sent out to the shortlisted applicants to invite them to attend an interview on a specific day and time. If you have to undertake a test this will be identified in the letter. Make sure you read the letter carefully, as it may say you have to confirm your attendance to the interview. Do you need to take anything with you? E.g. proof of identity, certificates as proof of qualifications, etc.

Interviews

At the interview there may be a panel of people who will ask you a number of questions each. There will always be one person that will chair the interview or open up the interview with introductions. They may also provide you with information on the terms and conditions of the employment. At the end of the interview they may ask if you have any questions. Make sure you have thought about what you need to know about them. Remember the interview is a two way process.

Job Offer

A job offer can be made subject to references. Once references have been received this will be formalised in writing. You would need to formally accept the offer in writing.

Start by making a list of all the things you need to think about and do to ensure you make effective job applications

....

....

....

....

....

Now imagine you have achieved getting that job, what next?

Well now you need to sustain yourself in that employment. You will at first feel out of your comfort zone as it is a new environment. You are now in the adult world. Being employed is different from being at school. You are accountable to your employer who wants good value for money and for you to work effectively has a member of the team who are working towards the same vision and aim for the benefit of the business.

Here is a list of what makes an effective employee:

- Considerate to other team members
- Supportive
- Caring
- Good communication
- Friendly working environment
- Everyone does their share of the work
- Reliable
- Trustworthy
- Honest
- Shows commitment
- Treats others with respect
- Flexible
- Contributes to new ideas
- Constructive

- Ability to adapt
- Organised
- Asked for help when you don't understand
- Listens carefully to instructions
- Motivated
- Always completes work on time
- Good time keeper
- Tries to solve problems
- Loyalty to the employer
- Clean & tidy
- Willing to learn
- Responsible attitude
- Gets on well with people
- Co-operates with supervisors
- Good team player

I'll take on this responsibility.

I'm right on time!

Now take a look at the list of qualities of an effective employee and write down the one's that you may need to develop further or look at improving

....

....

....

....

....

....

Looking at the list above now think about and write down what you would need to do to help you improve in these areas. Remember to put a date by the side when you want to achieve this by otherwise it may never happen.

....

....

....

....

....

....

....

You will need to make sure you strive to improve on the areas you have identified as this will help you with working more effectively and gaining the respect of your employer.

Chapter 9

Beating the Recession

Looking for a job during a recession can be a difficult time. I am constantly hearing people say there are no jobs. There are jobs but what they mean to say is that there are no jobs that are suitable for them. This can be that they are being too specific. Sometimes it is best to take any job rather than not have a job at all. If you are prepared to take any job you are likely to find something that you know you have the ability to do or feel comfortable doing.

Searching for jobs can be done in a variety of ways, Scouring the local and national papers, internet recruitment sites or a company sites or Jobcentre website. You have to be aware that some jobs are not advertised as recruitment costs to employers are expensive. So, people can be recruited by word of mouth so it may be someone that currently works there that knows someone. No matter what method of recruitment the employer chooses to use you will still have to complete an application form or submit a curriculum vitae.

Write a list here of the places you will search for jobs:

....

....

....

....

....

....

....

....

So how do you get to hear about the jobs that are not advertised? You can do this by networking.

What do I mean by networking?

Tell as many people as possible that you come into contact with that you are looking for a job. The more people you tell the more people there will be looking out for a job for you. Let me give you an example: You have 10 friends, your ten friends then tell another 10 people, and they then tell another 10 people. So far we now have 30 people that know that you are looking for a job.

That is 30 people that will now be on the lookout for jobs in shop windows, in the paper, hear someone in the local shop talking about a company taking on staff, etc., etc.

Write a list here of all the people you know that you could talk to about what you are looking for. This can be friends, relatives, neighbours, etc:

....

....

....

....

....

....

....

....

....

....

I bet you didn't realise you knew so many people that you could network with!

If you are going to be seriously looking for work you need to have a plan of action. As I have mentioned before you need to manage your time effectively. The more applications you make the more likely you are to get a job. It is no good just sitting there and waiting for something to happen as it won't. Nobody is going to wave a magic wand and hey presto you have a job. It is just not going to happen.

So here is an example of what I did when I was looking for work when I was made redundant.

First of all I became really organised at searching for jobs and completing the applications because I knew that it was just a numbers game; eventually something would give if I kept at it long enough. I had also started to look at the different opportunities open to me in relation to my knowledge, skills and experience. It was time to have a closer look at what I was capable of and stretch my imagination about other jobs I could apply for and try.

Remember all the different factors we have looked at throughout this book as they all have a part to play when you are searching for work. Here is a case study of how a young man called Arran that I worked with dealt with looking for work:

Arran was a young man who had just finished school and lacked in confidence. He had been looking for work in retail. He would go with his friends visiting shops looking for vacancies. He was doing all the right things but not getting the result he wanted. I started to coach him and we worked on his confidence as he always let his friends go first and ask about the jobs. Until I got him to realise that if there was a vacancy they may get the job. From this point he changed his behaviour became more confident and was always the first one into the shop to ask. Arran had a lot of good qualities but like most young people he couldn't see them and didn't share these qualities with potential employers. I helped Arran review his Curriculum Vitae to reflect his strengths and personal qualities. Within two weeks he had a job in a shop. Arran had perseverance, motivation and drive as he never let the knock backs stop him from carrying on and the determination that he would get a job. So when people say to you there are no jobs out there. There are and you just need to find them by doing what Arran did.

Now take time to think about what your plan is to look for a job and write it down here:

✎ ....

....

....

....

....

....

....

....

....

So now you have your plan it is down to you to put it into action. The sooner you get started the sooner you are likely to get a result.

Here are some top tips for you:

1. Maintain a positive mind and don't let the set backs hold you back. Just keep on going. Being positive means that you need to change the way you think and the language that you use. Sometimes we don't realise how negative this can be. Thinking negatively will not allow you to come across confidently to others and often will affect how you sell yourself to employers.

2. Plan your diary each week and decide where you are going to search for jobs. You have already written lists of where you could search, you need to be doing this on a regular basis.

3. Do you have self-belief? You need to believe in yourself. What is your belief at the moment about yourself? Is everything you think of the negative? Your brain will always think of the negatives easier than it will the positives. When your thoughts are negative and you start to put yourself down, stop and think. What evidence do you have to support this? Now change this thought into a positive.

4. Keeping motivated can be hard work when you search for jobs, especially when you can't find anything or when you go for interviews and don't get the job. What has helped you in the past with your motivation? What could you do to maintain your motivation? So keep up your spirits there is a job out there just for you. Focus on you getting that job by visualising yourself everyday being in that job. How good is that feeling when you are offered a job. Remember if you don't keep taking action then you will not move nearer to achieve your goal of getting a job.

5. If you could have an in the meantime job, what could it be? Find some temporary work as employers are more likely to employ you once you are employed than when you are not. Could you do some volunteer work?

Chapter 10

Recognising Your Strengths

Applying for jobs can be quite daunting; you may not know where to start. I want to help you overcome this. The first time I was made redundant I applied for thirty seven jobs and was invited to fourteen interviews. I found the more applications I wrote the easier it became as I was able to use information from other applications I had prepared. The jobs I applied for were not always my ideal job but I knew I had skills that were transferable and was able to demonstrate this on my job applications. So I want to help you to learn how to do this too.

Firstly, we are going to look at how to create the right impression with an employer when applying for a job or sending in a speculative curriculum vitae (CV). The key to this is understanding how to sell yourself to an employer. You need to see yourself as a product that an employer would want to buy. So this is about having self-awareness, self-belief and confidence. In this chapter we are going to take time to look at everything you have to offer an employer. The more awareness you have about yourself the more likely you are able to sell yourself to an employer.

So let's get started on this journey of self-exploration.

What do you know and notice about yourself?

What have you got to offer an employer?

Has that Gremlin suddenly come back into your head and produced all the negative thoughts or are you thinking positively?

In the first chapter you have already identified your hobbies and interests so that is a start as they will be things you are really good at.

Here are two boxes one of your strengths and one of your weaknesses. I have provided a list of words you can also add some of your own. Choose which box you would put them in for you:

Reliable   Work on own initiative
Good Time Keeper   Team Player
Organised   Communication Skills
Listening Skills   Motivated
Problem Solving   Friendly/Approachable
Sense of Humour   Attention to detail
Committed   Caring
Polite   Flexible
Enthusiastic   Ambitious
Helpful   Hard working

Strengths	Weaknesses

It is good to be aware of your strengths and weaknesses as this could be a question you are asked when you get to an interview. Knowing your weaknesses is also a good thing has once you are aware of them you can work on improving them to make them more of a strength.

Write down here the knowledge you have:

....

....

....

....

....

Write down here the experience you have:

E.g. Work placement, Saturday job, Voluntary work, baby sitting, paper round, etc

....

....

....

....

....

....

What are your areas of particular interest?

....

....

....

....

....

....

Can you now see that you have a lot to offer an employer? Do you now feel worthy to be able to get that job?

Now let's take a look at the language you use. People don't always realise that they have written something in negative language. You need to get used to recognising when you have demonstrated in your CV or job applications something in a negative way to an employer. Let me give you some examples:

Don't use negative statements	Use positive statements
I **feel** I am a good communicator.	I **am** a good communicator.
Even though **I failed to achieve my target**, I learned a great deal about Telesales.	Through this experience **I learned a great deal** about Telesales.
Some people have told me I have good communication skills.	**I have excellent** communication skills
I have had a **little** experience.	I have **relevant** experience.

In the past when I have been recruiting staff there have been many common mistakes people make when completing job applications. Some of these are as follows:

- They make assumptions that the employer will know they can do the job they are applying for by what they have identified in their employment history.
- They don't demonstrate on the job application their knowledge and skills in relation to what is laid out in the person specification.
- They don't provide examples to back up when they have used their knowledge and skills.

In my workshop 'How to Get Ahead and Get a Job' I help people to improve on how they structure their job applications and understand what an employer is looking for.

I don't want you to make the same mistakes that many people make, so if you follow my useful tips in this chapter you could be one step nearer to getting that job.

Useful tips on how to improve your Job Applications...

Here are some useful tips to help you improve your job applications:

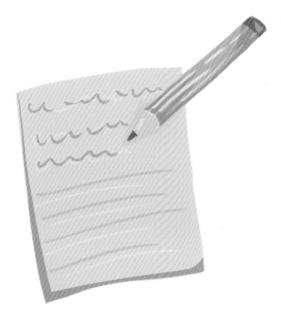

1. Firstly, start by writing down the different knowledge and skills you have gained in your life so far. Think about individual tasks you have been involved in. Are you giving yourself the credit for the abilities you have? You have already started to do this at the beginning of this chapter.

2. Read the person specification and job description carefully look at the language that is being used and use this in your job application.

3. The person specification is the criteria that will be used to shortlist you for an interview. Structure your application in the order it is on the person specification this will make it easier for the person undertaking the short listing. Answer each of the criteria providing examples to demonstrate your experience in this area.

4. Make sure you use positive language to demonstrate your abilities for example:

   'I have excellent communication skills'

   Now take another look at your job applications and see how you could improve what you have written using the tips above.

Curriculum Vitae

Applying for jobs with a CV is a little bit different from completing a job application. You can type up a CV as a template but you should always makes sure it reflects the job you are applying for or what the employer is asking for. If you are sending a speculative letter to an employer to see if there are any suitable vacancies you need to be clear what type of vacancy you would be interested in. To find out what an employer requires for a particular type of job, search on the internet for a similar job. Then use this information to make your CV more specific. See Chapter 14 from where you can find an example of a CV.

Also do your research on the internet for information about the employer. What type of company are they? What do they do? Find out as much as you can about them. When writing your covering letter make sure there is some reference to the company so it is specific to them and do a short paragraph on what you can offer them. You want them to move on to read your CV. See Chapter 14 from where you can find an example of a speculative letter. Remember to keep a copy of the CV and job applications you have sent off to employers.

Chapter 11

Preparing for Interviews

Job interviews are a way of employers finding out more about a number of individuals they are interested in to ensure they find the right person for the job. It is a two way process though as it is also about you finding out about them as an employer. The interview may consist of a face to face interview with a panel of people or one person interviewing you. You will be asked a series of questions to help them gather more information and find out more about you. What you are asked to do in addition to the interview will be dependant on the type of job you have applied for. For example, if it is an administrative job you may be asked to undertake a task on a computer. Some interviews may ask for a presentation, group exercise written tests, etc. This would be explained in the letter inviting you for an interview.

If you have never had an interview for a job before then you may have mixed emotions. You may feel a bit anxious or even excited as you don't know what to expect. So dealing with how you feel about it is important. You need to not let your nerves or fear get the better of you. Any negative emotion that you have will affect how you may perform in the interview. If you are nervous your mind may go blank and you will not be able to answer the questions to the best of your ability.

Well imagine today that you have just received that letter inviting you for an interview for that job you have always wanted. Initially you may feel excited after a few hours you may feel the fear creeping in. So let me help you deal with this. Do you remember the chapter on self-belief right now this is what you need to have.

Start now by writing down 3 positive beliefs you have in relation to the interview:

Start each sentence I believe...

1.

2.

3.

Now you have your beliefs you need to read these in a morning and on an evening. This will start to work on the negative thoughts within you and maintain a positive outlook on the interview and how you will perform.

You need to make sure you portray yourself to the employer that you are confident. Stand in front of a mirror and check out your body language. Do you think you look confident or are your shoulders drooping?

Stand tall hold your shoulders back, eye contact and read out your beliefs. Listen to the tone in your voice as you read them out do you sound confident? Do you sound like you believe what you are saying? If you can also check out your body language when you are seated, remember you will be sitting down in front of the employer.

What other preparation do you need to do?

Choose outfit – don't leave this right until the last minute as you may need to have your suit dry cleaned or clothes need to be washed and ironed. Try it on does it make you feel good? If you feel good in what you are wearing this is a great start for the interview?

Hair cut – Make sure if you need to get your hair cut that you have booked your appointment in time for the interview. You need to create a good impression for the employer. Being clean and tidy is important.

Ring and confirm attending interview – Only do this if this is requested in the letter you received. Check your letter to see if that has been asked of you.

Find out bus times – Check your appointment time in your letter and identify the bus that will only make you arrive on time. As public transport can be late look for the bus prior to this to give yourself enough time. Also make sure you take into consideration that traffic may be bad or that you may have a walk from the bus stop to where the interview is.

Read application – You need to read the copy of the job application that you sent to the employer. Look at the person specification and try and imagine what types of question the employer may ask you. Make notes on a notepad. You can take the notepad into the interview with you in case you are nervous and then you can just say in the interview 'I will just have to refer to my notes'. Remember you got the interview on the basis of what you put in your job application so you need to make sure you say in the interview what you have said in your application.

Decide what you need to know from employer - Write down questions to ask employer on a notepad. It is so easy to forget what you want to know. Look through the information they sent you with the job application does it tell you the following:
- Salary
- Holidays
- Hours of work
- Pension

Think why you have applied for the job/Why you want to work for this organisation – this may be asked in the interview so you need to feel prepared and don't want to get caught out. Here are some examples:

I would enjoy the job as I feel it would be a challenge.

I am interested in the work that your company does.

I have looked on your website and I have noticed that... and that is of particular interest to me.

Decide what would successful mean to you - I don't want you to be disappointed if you don't get the job. You will only beat yourself up afterwards. You need to view the interview as a learning experience. So let's define what would be a successful interview for you. Here are some examples:

- Answered all questions confidently
- Felt relaxed and calm throughout

Now write your definition down here:

....

....

....

DAY OF INTERVIEW

Get up early – Make sure you set your alarm clock so you get you early so you are not rushing and can take your time getting ready. If you end up rushing this will start to make you panic and stressed, creating negative feelings.

Be organised – Make sure you have everything they have requested you take with to the interview e.g. passport, certificates of proof of qualifications, etc.

Stay relaxed and calm - Take deep breaths this helps the body to relax. Tell yourself you are confident. Believe in yourself.

Arrive on time - Give plenty of time for your journey allowing for traffic and the walking distance. If you have to rush this will make you panic. When you arrive turn off your mobile phone or put it on silent. There is nothing worse than when your mobile rings in the middle of an interview. You may also lose your train of thought if you are just in the middle of responding to a question.

Listen carefully to the questions – Make sure you answer them fully. If you are not sure you can ask them to repeat the question again just to check this out. Be polite and smile. Relax and let your personality show.

It is important to understand what makes a good interview and what makes a bad interview. See the lists below:

WHAT MAKES A GOOD INTERVIEW?	WHAT MAKES A BAD INTERVIEW?
<ul><li>Answer questions in a confident and firm voice</li><li>Answer all questions with detail</li><li>Provide examples</li><li>Keeping to the point</li><li>Maintain eye contact with the interviewers</li><li>Sit upright in the chair</li><li>Never lie</li><li>Remember what you have put in your job application</li><li>Say what you have put in your job application</li><li>Showing enthusiasm for the job</li><li>Be passionate about the work</li><li>Good preparation</li><li>Research</li></ul>	<ul><li>Answers were too general</li><li>Inappropriate dress</li><li>Struggle to answer common interview questions</li><li>Nervous</li><li>Unfocused</li><li>Arrived late</li><li>Too pushy</li><li>Lack of rapport with the person interviewing</li><li>Unable to answer questions</li><li>Mind goes blank</li></ul>

AFTER THE INTERVIEW

If you are unsuccessful here are some tips for you for next time:

Ask for feedback - If you are unsuccessful in the interview ask for feedback so you can look at where you need to improve next time. Remember every unsuccessful interview is one step closer to getting a job. **Don't give up**.

Assess what you could do next time – reflect on your feedback from the interview and also your own thoughts and decide what you need to do to ensure you improve at the next interview.

Continue to take action – If you don't take any action and continue to apply for jobs you are no longer in the game. Don't let the experience of the interview knock you back. Stay positive and motivated.

Chapter 12

Exploring Setting up a Business

You may be involved in school in developing an enterprise with a group of friends in school. This can be great for starting to get you to think of whether you would like to set up a business. I have visited schools in the past where young people had come up with some great imaginative ideas for businesses and were making it make money for them.

Remember setting up and running a business is not an easy option as you have to work hard to achieve a successful business but the benefits and rewards can be far greater than being employed by someone else. So let's take a look at some of the advantages and disadvantages of being self-employed.

Advantages	Disadvantages
Be your own boss	May work longer hours initially
Only have yourself to answer to	Hard work to build up business reputation
Every decision made by you	Inconsistent income
Independence	Earn less in the short term
Freedom	No holiday pay
Flexible	No sickness pay
Reap the rewards of your own efforts	Earn no income in business whilst on holiday
Sense of achievement	A risk
Pay less tax than being employed	Stressful
Choose who you want to work with	Relationships with clients make or break your business
Have total control over your career	More responsibility
Focus on what you like doing the most	Need ability to be multi-skilled
Boosts your confidence	No one to keep you on track or motivated
Job satisfaction	Isolation is working on your own

Look at the list of advantages and disadvantages. Do the advantages outweigh the disadvantages for you?

You need to be multi-skilled to be self-employed. In the beginning you need to be able to do everything yourself, e.g. administration, accounts, marketing, providing your service, etc. Once your business is successful you may be able to pay someone else to do some of these tasks for you. So there are many different skills, qualities and attributes that you will need if you are to be successful in self-employment.

Below is a list of skills, qualities and attributes. Circle the ones you think you have.

Motivation	Determination	Passion
Drive	Organised	Charismatic
Enthusiasm	Time Management	Good communicator
Helpful	Honest	Trustworthy
Reliable	Finance	Marketing
Visionary	Focused	Self-discipline
Commitment	Energy	Willingness to take risks
Creativity	Customer orientated	Computer literate
Positive attitude	Problem solver	Patient
Responsible	Conscientious	Leadership

You will not be good at all of these but it is about you recognising the ones that are your strengths. You can then develop an awareness of how you can deal with the ones you have as a weakness.

Now you have looked at the advantages, disadvantages, skills and attributes is setting up a business an option for you?

You need to be clear as to why you would like to set up a business.

Write a list here as to the reasons why you are considering setting up a business

....

....

....

To move forward with setting up a business you need to make sure you can overcome any fear you may have, have confidence and self-belief in yourself and your idea, finding the right kind of support to help you move forward.

Here are some useful tips for you when you decide to set up a business:

- Identify the fears that may stop you moving forward. If you don't overcome these you will not achieve what you want to achieve.

This business will probably fail. Don't even try!

- Have a clear plan and focus on this. Make time to take the actions required to move you closer to your plan. Remember **Time + Effort = Success**.

- Tell people about your business. Don't give away too many secrets though.

- Have confidence in your idea and your ability to succeed. Every success you have will build up your confidence.

- Don't allow any setbacks to knock your confidence. Keep going and never give up.

- Maintain a positive outlook and attitude.

- Have self-belief in you and your business. Maintain this by keeping a success diary. When things aren't going to plan remind yourself of your successes.

....

....

....

....

....

If you still think self-employment is for you the next question will try and find the creativity and passion within you.

Do you have an idea for your business? What is the vision for your business? Who will your customers be?

....

....

....

....

....

....

....

....

....

If you have a clear idea about your business you are one step nearer to having what you want. For those of you that may not have identified anything you may need to take a little longer to think about this.

- Talk to positive people who will give you the inspiration to keep you going.

- Find the right kind of support for yourself that maintains your motivation and keeps the enthusiasm alive in you.

- Check to see if business start up funding available. Princes Trust does support young people setting up businesses so check out their website and the contact in the local area.

Chapter 13

Making Choices Going to University/College

You may decide that you want to go to university or college, to be educated in a particular subject to further your career. The college will provide you with the knowledge and skills to have a trade for a particular job, e.g. plumber, electrician, care assistant, administration. You may also get the opportunity to be taken on as an apprentice to use your new found knowledge and skills. The university will provide you with a higher level of qualification opening up a broad range of career opportunities which you can check out when researching the different courses.

Choosing to go to university is a big decision that is life changing and can be an enjoyable experience. Going to university can be expensive so you need to know that you are making the right choice. Not just because of the cost but to ensure you can achieve the career you want.   College is a less expensive option but can still be as life changing and just as enjoyable. At university and college you will have an opportunity to study something you have a real passion and interest in, as well as being able to take part in the great social life and make new friends. There are many universities to choose from in different towns and cities offering a broad range of subjects. Colleges also offer a broad range of courses local to where you live.

At the beginning of this book I told you about my experience of choosing a job that my parents wanted me to do and also about my son who chose to go to university to study law to become a Solicitor. Both of these choices we made were not right for us.   So think very carefully about the choice you are making ask yourself this question

'Will it help you to achieve the career you want and is it what you want and not what someone else is telling you to do?'

Remember this is the starting point of your life the life you will have in the future. It has to be right for you not about living someone else's dream. My next question is

'Do you have a real passion and interest for the subjects you will study?'

Working towards doing a degree you will be at university for at least three years. College courses can be less than this.   Do you want to spend time studying something you have no or little interest in? Studying can be interesting if you find the right course for you in relation to your chosen career.

To find out what is right for you do your research. There are more than 40,000 full-time courses.   You need to keep an open mind as to which university you would like to study at.

So, which universities appeal to you, write them down here:

....

....

....

....

....

Now you have identified the university you are interested in you can visit their websites and obtain more detailed information.   Here are is a list of what you need to check out:

- Requirements against your predicted grades.
- Courses with the same name can differ hugely between universities, look at what each one offers.
- Combined courses.
- Course's employability ratings -does it offer work placements/ internships
- Do they do open days
- How many hours teaching
- Assessment – exam, assignment, thesis, etc
- Support available – personal tutor

You can also use the above to research for the courses that colleges offer.

So, which courses immediately grab your imagination and attention?

....

....

....

....

....

Which course would give you a sustainable source of stimulation and enjoyment for the length of your study?

....

....

....

....

....

....

Don't forget to attend the open days as you will get to find out more about the university the location, what it offers, is it a quiet campus and the cost of living of the area. You will get to know if it feels right for you. Open days at local colleges will help you to find out more about what is on offer and whether it is the right course for you.

Make sure once you have made your decision you know what the process is for applying and when you will need to submit your application.

Chapter 14
Resources

This section will provide you with information on websites that support some of the information provided within this book. It will also provide you with templates or tools to help you with your development and getting the best to help you achieve the future you want.

Recognising Your Strengths

Curriculum Vitae Templates/Cover Letters

http://jobsearch.about.com/od/cvsamples/a/cvtemplate.htm

https://nationalcareersservice.direct.gov.uk/advice/getajob/cvs/Pages/default.aspx

Preparing for Interviews

http://www.prospects.ac.uk/interview_tips_preparing_yourself.htm

http://jobsearch.about.com/od/interviewsnetworking/ss/job-interview.htm

Exploring Setting up a Business

Information for young people setting up a business –

http://www.princes-trust.org.uk/need_help/enterprise_programme.aspx

http://sbinformation.about.com/od/startingabusiness/a/How-To-Start-A-Business.htm

How to get started - http://www.hmrc.gov.uk/startingup/index.htm

Making Choices Going to University or College

Useful info for parents on the BBC website -
http://www.bbc.co.uk/schools/parents/helping_choose_a_course_and_university/
Link on the left hand side to post 16 qualifications for info on choosing a course at college.

This is written for a student audience - http://www.push.co.uk/

UCAS is the official guide - http://www.ucas.ac.uk/students/choosingcourses/

Link to league tables - http://www.ucas.com/students/choosingcourses/choosinguni/

Provides important dates -http://www.ucas.com/students/importantdates

For students - http://www.studential.com/applying/choosing-the-right-degree

Articles and discussion forum - http://www.thestudentroom.co.uk

PRINCES TRUST

www.princes-trust.org.uk

Conclusion

You have now got everything you need to get you started in planning the future that you want. You will be able to make decisions and choices feeling totally informed having worked through the processes. Hopefully you will be filled with the confidence and self-belief that you will need to take you forward to the future this will have been proved to you through the exercises you have undertaken. You have also been provided with resources to help you further. I would like to wish you all the best in you achieving the result you want in your future and on your journey along the way.

Good luck.

Sandra Greatorex

I have helped a lot of people that have been long term unemployed as well as those under the threat of redundancy. This was the work I had a passion about as I understand the struggle of finding work and the stress and anxiety it causes when you are unemployed. After being made redundant twice I knew I had a passion of wanting to help people to survive this difficult situation.

I have provided unemployed people with advice and support to help them focus on a positive outlook, maintain their motivation and improve CV's and job applications. I have designed workshops to help them personally develop to improve their employability. One-to-one life coaching sessions also help them to strengthen what they have learned. Within different roles I was responsible for recruiting new staff and supporting existing staff to enhance their skills and development.

Some of the clients I have supported have been young people who have been trying to get a job that gets them on the first rung of the ladder. In schools I have been asked to assess young people with their interview skills, which has helped them become aware of how they could improve. I worked as a Youth Worker for twelve years helping young people to prepare for life and building up their confidence.

My coaching and consultancy business helps individuals who have been made redundant or been long term unemployed to get back into work whether that is to re-define their career or options that are open to them or get back into the work they know. Employability is of interest to me and particularly assisting and supporting young people who sometimes struggle to recognise the qualities, knowledge and skills they have to offer in their future career. I have undertaken coaching with young people to help them to collate a well presented Curriculum Vitae.

After working through this book you will be prepared for the decisions and choices of future life and will be more than capable of being able to follow the chosen path.

Butterfly Transformation Ltd

Mobile: 07967 205506

Email: info@butterflytransform.co.uk

Website: www.butterflytransform.co.uk

Twitter: infobutterfly

Are you worried about your future?

Are you concerned you are not going to get a job?

Does your mind go blank when people ask what you want to do?

Would you like some support in helping you to make the right decisions?

This book is aimed at young people who are going to have to make decisions and choices about their future. It will help you to identify the journey for the future, whatever route you choose to take.

Sandra Greatorex designed this step-by-step process to help you to get started on your future career whatever route you choose. It will take you through some practical exercises which will help you to explore what you want and where you would like to be in the future.

Take responsibility for your life and decide on your options that will help you to move towards your future.

transformation & growth for life

Illustrations by Sarah Bradley

ISBN 978-1-903568-76-7